D0375841
Girl's
Handbook to
Friendship
Fiona Foden

First published in 2013, by Scholastic Children's Books
Euston House, 24 Eversholt Street,
London NW1 1DB, UK

A division of Scholastic Ltd
www.scholastic.com
London ~ New York ~ Toronto ~ Sydney ~ Auckland
Mexico City ~ New Delhi ~ Hong Kong

ISBN 978-1-4351-5027-0

Manufactured in Singapore
Lot #
2 4 6 8 10 9 7 5 3 1
08/13

Girl's Handbook *to* Friendship

Contents

Where Would You be Without Friends?

They share the good times and always make you smile – no doubt about it, nothing is better than being with your best friends. This book is all about making the most of your amazing friendships – from showing your buddies how much you care, to coping with those awkward moments (because even the closest friendships can get complicated sometimes). Read on to make sure your friends are for keeps...

Ten Friendship Commandments

Remember these and you'll always be a great friend…

Today I'm making a promise to...

1 Never take my friends for granted

2 Stay in touch no matter how busy I am

3 Never gossip about a friend (because I know how hurt I'd be)

4 Always be there for my friends when they're feeling low

5 Make sure my friends always feel included

6 Be a good listener

7 Keep my friends' secrets close to my heart

8 Encourage my friends and celebrate their successes

9 Stick up for a friend if someone's being mean

10 Always let my buddies know how fantastic they are

What Kind of Friend Are You?

"I have the greatest friends in the world and they're real . . . I trust them."

Anne Hathaway, actor

Revealing quiz

What makes you a fabulous friend?

Discover what makes you a top-notch friend with these six quick questions...

1 You're getting ready for a party together and your friend's taking forever to decide what to wear. What do you do?

a. Encourage her to be more adventurous with her look
b. Let her take as much time as she needs
c. Reassure her that she'll look amazing whatever she wears

2 Your friend has to do a performance in front of the whole school and is feeling nervous. How do you help her?

a. By practicing together and making it fun
b. By talking over *why* she's nervous, and helping to build her confidence
c. By encouraging her to just go for it and do her best

3 What's your favorite way of spending time with friends?

a. Telling each other jokes and funny stories
b. Having deep chats and sharing secrets
c. Sharing dreams for the future

4 Your friend seems a bit blue today. How do you try to lift her spirits?

a. By doing something fun together to help her forget her worries
b. By talking things over and figuring out what she's sad about
c. By trying to help her see that her problem isn't such a biggie after all

5 What's the worst thing a friend can do to you?

a. Refuse to join in when I suggest doing something fun or silly
b. Blab a secret
c. Act weird or distant without explaining why

6 Which of the following describes your perfect sleepover?

a. Lots of friends plus some comedy movies
b. Just one or two close friends, chatting late into the night
c. I like having a theme – like doing hairstyles or making pizzas

Conclusions

Mostly As...

You're a Bubbly Buddy

You're always up for a laugh – no wonder you're so popular. While you love your best friend, you're also open to meeting new people too. Everyone enjoys being with you because you're full of crazy ideas and such fun to be with.

Friends love you because: Life's always sparkly when you're around.

Mostly Bs...

You're a Magical Friend

Why magical? Because you're kind, thoughtful and always make friends feel good. If a friend has a problem, you always know how to sort things out. You're wise, clever and caring – no wonder your friends think you're a star!

Friends love you because: You're a great listener and always let them know you care.

Mostly Cs...

You're a Forever Friend

Full of ideas for new things to do, you're the kind of friend who makes life exciting. You somehow bring out the best in people too, helping them to feel more confident. Loyalty is hugely important to you – and you believe a true friendship is for keeps.

Friends love you because: They know you'll always be there for them.

What friends are for

Friends are fun to hang out with – but they can also give you so much more. In your close circle, who fits the following roles?

The good listener: She's the one you confide in and has time for everyone.

The stylish one: Fashionable and cool, she helps you make up your mind when you're unsure of your look.

The problem-solver: Sometimes, looking at a situation from someone else's point of view can help you decide what to do.

The funny girl: She has everyone shaking with laughter.

The confidence-booster: She helps you to believe in yourself, even if you're feeling unsure.

The sunny one: Some friends just know how to lift your mood.

The adventurous one: She'll encourage you to set goals for yourself, and go for what you want in life.

The mind-reader: You know each other so well, it's almost as if she can tell what you're thinking.

Best friend or big group ... what's right for you?

While some girls can't imagine being without a best friend, others feel happier with a wide circle of friends and like them all equally. The great thing about a best friend is that she knows you so well, and completely "gets" your sense of humour. But life can feel a little lonely if she's away, or can't see you for some reason.

When you have several friends – or a big gang – chances are there's always someone to hang out with. Plus, you're not relying on one person so much. But even if you hang out with lots of different people, there's probably an "inner circle" you're closest to. Remember that friendships are always slightly changing, and it's normal to feel closer to one friend at certain times, and someone else at others.

So, do best friends rule, or should you hang out with a group? It's up to you to decide. All that matters is that you feel comfortable and do what feels right for *you*.

Smart Girl Talk

Should I have a best friend?

There can be a lot of pressure to have a best friend. You might feel you're missing out if you don't have one at the moment – but the thing to remember is that close friendships develop naturally. You can do lots of things to meet and get to know people, but you can't *make* it happen.

You might feel completely happy having a group of friends rather than one best friend. If you do want a best friend, just be as open and friendly as you can – but remember that you can still get that "best friend feeling" from a group of friends who know you really well.

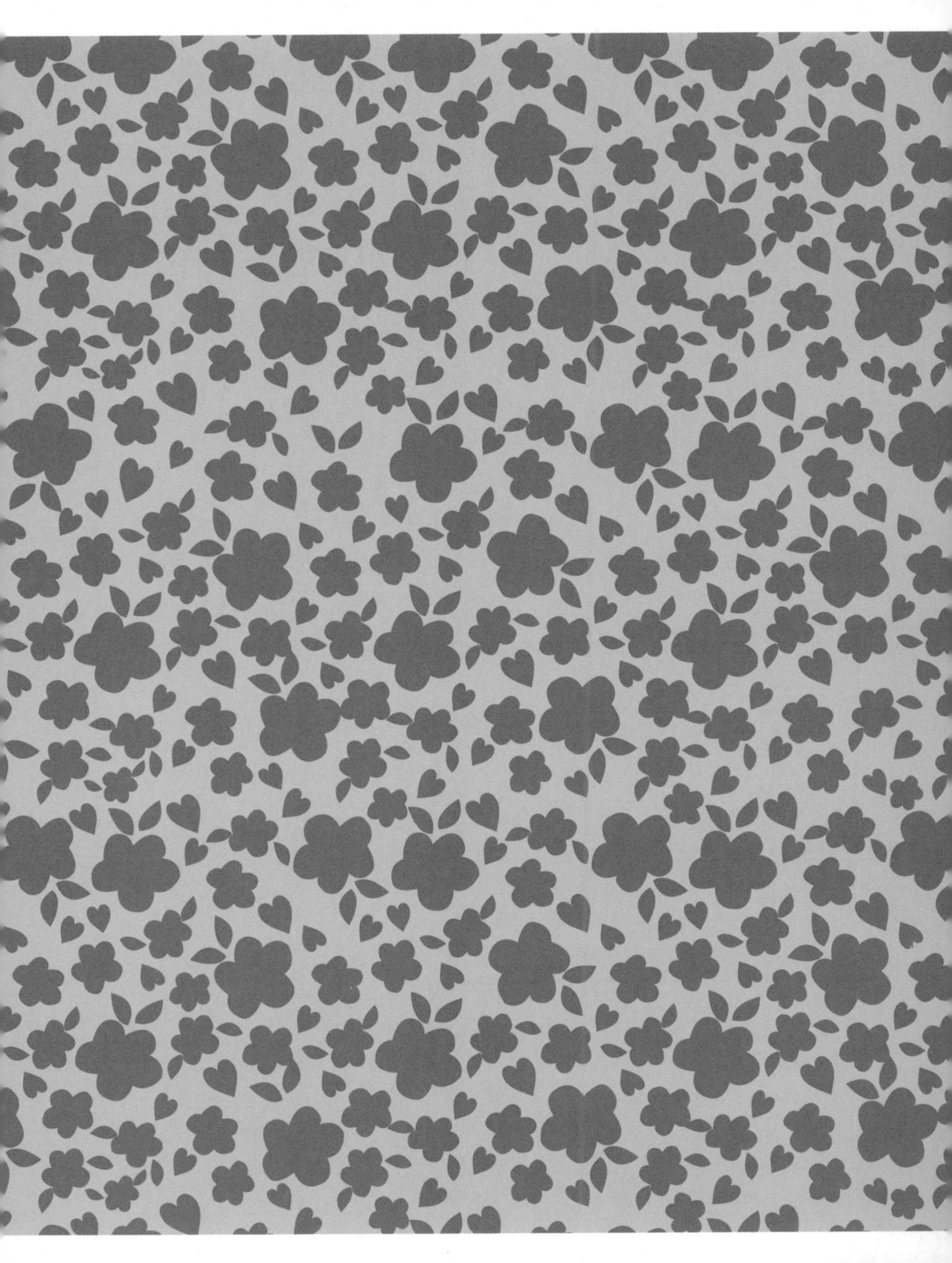

"I love my friends ... I love sitting with them and listening to their stories."

Beyoncé, singer

How to be the world's best buddy

It's those little thoughtful things you do that make all the difference...

If your friend seems sad...

She might want to talk about it, or she may not even know why she feels blue. If something's worrying her, you'll soon be able to tell if she wants to share it. If she does, then take time to listen and make some gentle suggestions. Even if she doesn't feel like confiding in you right now, you're helping her just by being there and showing you care.

When she's done something amazing...

One of the best things about friendship is having someone to celebrate with. Tell her how happy and proud you are of her, even if you feel a twinge of envy (which is natural, by the way). Is there anything you can learn from her? A friend's successes can make you strive harder and reach for your dreams. That doesn't mean you have to be hugely competitive with her though. But a super-clever or talented friend can inspire you to do your best.

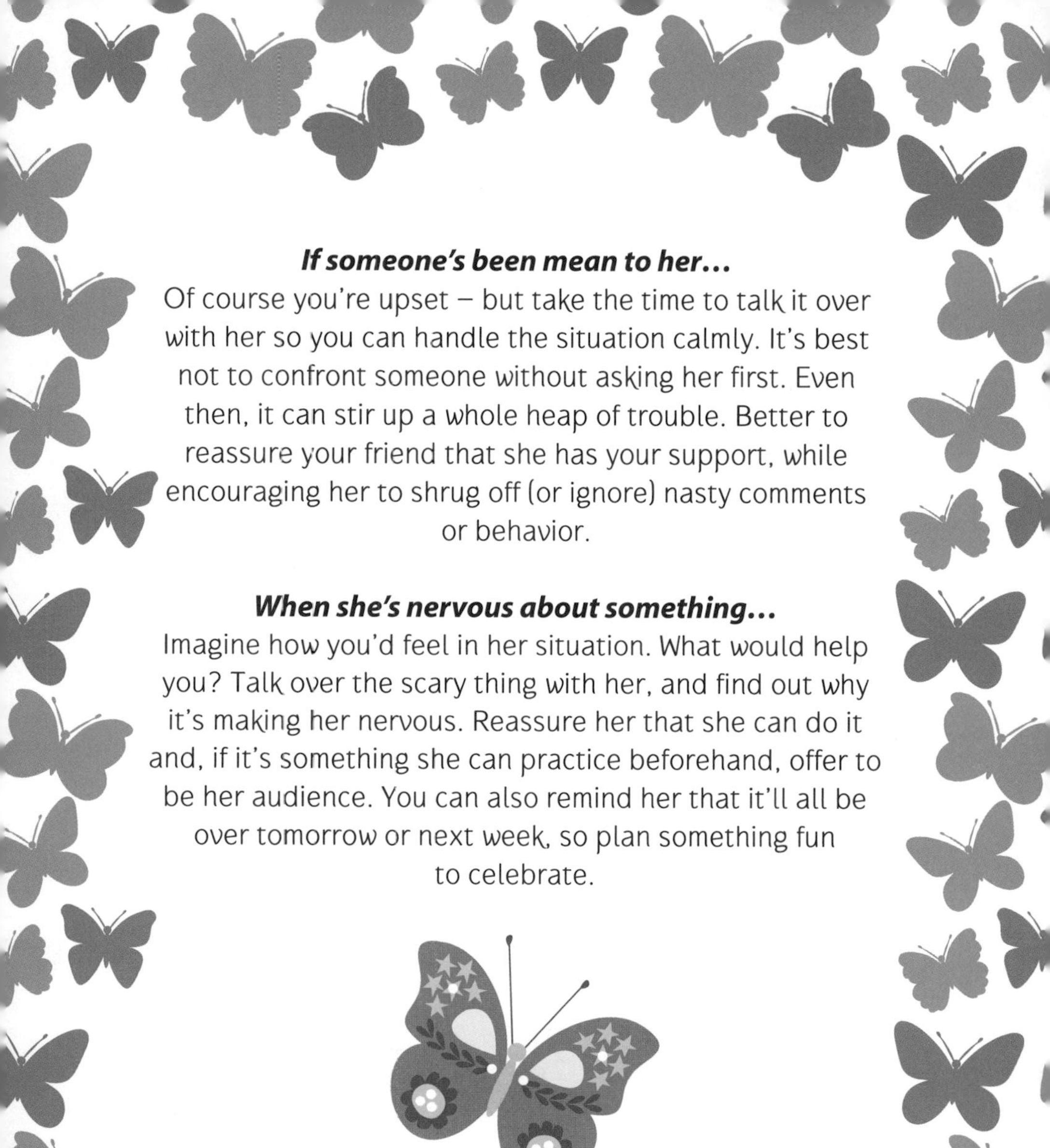

If someone's been mean to her...

Of course you're upset – but take the time to talk it over with her so you can handle the situation calmly. It's best not to confront someone without asking her first. Even then, it can stir up a whole heap of trouble. Better to reassure your friend that she has your support, while encouraging her to shrug off (or ignore) nasty comments or behavior.

When she's nervous about something...

Imagine how you'd feel in her situation. What would help you? Talk over the scary thing with her, and find out why it's making her nervous. Reassure her that she can do it and, if it's something she can practice beforehand, offer to be her audience. You can also remind her that it'll all be over tomorrow or next week, so plan something fun to celebrate.

When she asks your opinion on an outfit…

If it suits her, then it's easy – part of being a friend is boosting her confidence by telling her how great she looks. But if you really feel her look isn't working, try to let her know in a positive way. You could say, "It's nice, but it might work better if you wore that top with those other pants instead. Why don't you try it and see?"

If she's moving or going to a new school…

Show her you care by telling her you'll miss her – but try not to be too tearful or miserable, as that'll make her feel worse. Instead, talk about the good things you'll get out of going to different schools – like you'll have loads more to talk about. It's a good idea to arrange something for her to look forward to (like a sleepover or a shopping day together) so she can see that your friendship will stay rock solid.

When your friend has a serious problem

As a good friend, you'll listen and do whatever you can to help. But sometimes a friend's problem is too serious for you to take on all by yourself. It can start affecting you too, keeping you awake at night and making your school work suffer. The best thing to do is to talk to an adult you can trust – someone who'll handle it calmly and know what to do. Never feel you're carrying a big problem all on your own.

Ten ways to show you care

When you're extra-busy it's easy for the days to slip by without getting in touch. Here's how to remind your friend that she's special to you…

1 You don't have to spend much (or anything at all) for a gift to feel special. It's more important that it's just right for her – one of those "I saw this and thought of you" presents.

2 Make her a playlist to suit her mood or situation – for instance, chilled-out tunes if she's studying hard, or happy songs to get her in a holiday mood.

3 If she's feeling *bleurgh*, offer to help her do her hair or create a new look from clothes already hiding in her wardrobe. Or you could invite her over for a manicure, setting out all your polishes and letting her pick her favorites.

4 Bake her favorite cupcakes or cookies, pack them beautifully in a tissue-lined box, and pop around to share them with her.

5 Try writing a song together. Even if it's not destined for chart success, you'll have fun figuring out the melody and lyrics (and no one else needs to hear it!).

6 Home-made cards are special because they're unique – and they're not just for birthdays either. Why not make one to say "well done", "you're great" or "thinking of you"?

7 Make a note of when she's about to do something important or brave, and send her a good luck text. Remember to call or text afterwards too, to see how it went. You can also organize something fun to do now the pressure's off.

8 If you think she looks great, or love her style, don't forget to compliment her.

9 Don't always decide what you'll do together. Sometimes it's nice to let her choose.

10 Leave a sweet note for her to find later in her bedroom. You can keep it simple: something like, "You always make me smile", will make her *smile* too.

Tricky Moments and Fall-outs

"I like friends who are honest and loyal."

Vanessa Hudgens, actor

Handling a friendship blip

Disagreements and fall-outs are upsetting – but they happen to everyone sometimes. Often, a friendship wobble is caused by something tiny that you can both get over pretty quickly. If you can, it's best to put it behind you and focus on your friend's many good points. After all, no one's perfect. Everyone has weird moods or says things without thinking occasionally. Brushing the blip aside, and being firm friends again, feels far better than holding a grudge.

AGONY AUNT

Your friendship hiccups solved...

Q. My friend wants me to do something risky. If I say no, she'll think I'm boring – what should I do?
A. If something scares you or makes you feel uncomfortable, don't do it. A quick, 'No, I don't want to do that', is better than a pile of excuses. You might worry that she'll think you're not as daring as she is, but that doesn't matter. Having the courage to speak your mind and not give in to pressure is something to be truly proud of.

Q. At first I was flattered that my friend copies my style, but now it's really annoying me. Should I let her know?
A. It is flattering – but yes, it can also be irritating if someone seems to be stealing your ideas. Rather than confronting her, try to work out why she's doing it. Does she lack confidence? Or is she just following fashion, rather than a style you've put together yourself? Encourage her to create her own look by having a trying-on session together. If you help her to feel good about herself, she'll soon develop her own personal style.

Q. I love my friend but she seems to want me all to herself. If I talk to anyone else at break, she gets jealous. What can I do?

A. It's great to feel wanted but sometimes it can go too far. However close you are, she shouldn't try to control you or decide who you can and can't talk to. People usually behave like this because they feel insecure. Explain that she's really important to you, but that you can chat to other people if you like. As a caring friend, it's good to help her to feel included, but don't feel pressured to stay by her side all the time.

Q. My friend has blabbed a secret and I'm so upset. Why did she do this?

A. Secrets can spill out of mouths by accident - but even so, it's not OK. Tell your friend you know she's blabbed, giving her a chance to explain why. Maybe she didn't realize she was supposed to keep it to herself. Or perhaps she couldn't resist passing it on. If so, you can still be friends - but don't tell her anything you wouldn't want other people to know. Some friends just aren't that good at keeping secrets.

Q. My friend is always asking to copy my homework. How should I deal with it?

A. First, remind her that teachers usually know when homework's been copied. Everyone makes little mistakes, and if the same ones appear in hers, it's a dead giveaway. More importantly, try to find out why she wants to copy. Is she just disorganized and forgets to do it? If so, try to help her sort out a system so she writes homework tasks in her diary and has somewhere tidy to work. If she's just being lazy, it's not really fair that she expects you to do the work for her.

Q. I don't mind a bit of friendly teasing but sometimes my friend takes it too far. How can I get her to stop?

A. Friends can say upsetting things without meaning it, especially if the two of you often make jokey remarks. But if it's more 'ouch' than funny, tell her you find that comment a bit hurtful or upsetting. You can make it less of a big deal by adding, 'I'm probably just feeling a bit tired and sensitive.' Hopefully, she'll be more thoughtful next time.

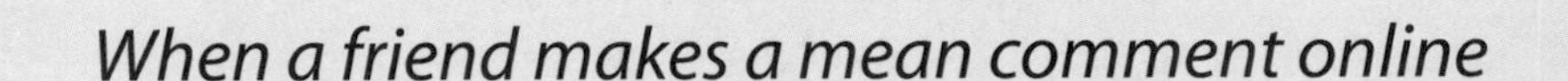

When a friend makes a mean comment online

When you're used to chatting online – or texting – it's easy to forget that words can take on a slightly different meaning or emphasis when they're written down (especially when they're public). For instance, it's easier to tell if someone's joking by the tone of their voice, their facial expressions or even their body language. Written words can seem more harsh than they were intended to be.

Before you do anything, take a moment to think what your friend actually meant. As long as it's not too serious, you needn't make a huge drama out of it or involve other friends. Just say something like, "When I read that, I felt a bit hurt and wondered why you said it?" By giving her the chance to explain, you're being fair and keeping your cool. If a comment is downright nasty, then don't respond – and do tell a parent, or another adult you can trust.

I can't help feeling jealous of my friend!

So she has amazing vacations, and a gorgeous bedroom filled with every gadget imaginable? It's natural to feel a bit jealous. Try not to let it spoil your friendship, though. Whenever you have an envy attack, remind yourself of all the things you have – maybe parents who have plenty of time for you, or lots of friends who are fun to be with. They're far more important than the latest gadget, which will soon stop being the must-have thing anyway. Having expensive possessions doesn't mean she's happier than you are. Plus, there are probably things she secretly envies about you too.

Who's who in your friendship circle?

It takes all sorts to make a gang of friends – in fact, it's the mix that keeps things interesting. Spot anyone *you* know?

The Leader

She's great at making things happen and bringing everyone together. Although she can seem a bit bossy, remember she still feels insecure sometimes, just like everyone else. So don't assume she has rock-solid confidence.

The Peace-keeper

This sweet soul might not be the loudest – but she helps to bond the group together. Her talent is for helping people to get along, and she's definitely missed when she's not there.

The Yes-girl

She's the easy-going girl who is rarely decisive, preferring to go along with the crowd. Don't underestimate her, though – she has hidden strengths, and is no doormat.

The Joker

She adds life and sparkle to the group, and helps to dispel any small disagreements. While she might feel she's expected to be happy all the time, there'll be times when she feels more serious or sensitive, just like everyone else.

The Deep-thinker

Often quieter than the rest, she still holds her own with her wit and intelligence. You know you can trust and confide in her.

The Organizer

She'd rather have a firm plan than just "let things happen" and can be a little controlling – but this is only because she wants everything to run smoothly. She always has her friends' best interests at heart.

The Dreamer

You may think she's on another planet sometimes – and yes, she sometimes lives in a world of her own. She's also hugely creative, full of ideas and smarter than many people think.

The New Girl

She's finding her feet and quietly sussing everyone out to work out where she fits in. Be sure to include her, as it may take a while for her courage to grow and her true personality to shine through.

Here comes trouble...

Occasionally, one person in your friendship group seems intent on stirring up trouble. What not to do: gang up against her or force her out. She might have problems or worries that are making her behave this way, so perhaps you can gently try to find out what's wrong.

If she's still upsetting you and the others, distance yourself a little, while still being friendly and polite. It's likely that she just wants attention, or is annoyed because everyone isn't doing what she wants. In situations like this, it's best to rise above it and act normally, as if nothing's going on. Of course, if she's behaving really badly or bullying, then tell her to stop – and have a chat with an adult you trust.

Why it's good to forgive

A fall-out needn't mean the end of your friendship. Sometimes people do things without thinking them through, and it's a shame to lose a good friend over something petty or trivial. So, rather than giving her the cold shoulder, have a chat to try and find out what's happened. Be honest – but don't make a big issue out of it.

If you're still annoyed, ask yourself: is this really important, or can I let it go? If hanging out again feels a little strange at first, your friend might just be feeling awkward. Doing something fun together can help to break the ice, and remind both of you that a good friendship is too precious to lose over a small disagreement.

How to say sorry

No one's perfect, and sometimes you might have upset a friend by accident. So what should you do?

Don't avoid her. It might seem easier right now, but the sooner you can make things right again, the better.

Do apologize if you know you were in the wrong. It takes a lot of courage, and your friend will respect you for being honest and brave.

Don't babble a pile of excuses, or try to pass the blame onto someone else. It'll just make things trickier and involve other people, and be harder to sort out.

Do tell your friend if it was a mistake or misunderstanding. And if something happened to make you behave that way, then tell her that too (for example, "I'm sorry, know I was thoughtless. It's not an excuse, but I've had a lot going on in my life lately"). Explaining things as clearly as you can will help to rebuild the trust between you.

Don't make yourself feel worse by dwelling on what's happened. Apologize, put it behind you and get on with being friends again.

Do act like your normal, cheerful self once it's been dealt with. No need to keep on apologizing over and over.

Don't bombard her with texts, calls or presents to try and make it up to her. It'll just make the situation feel more pressured.

Do remember that no one's perfect, and it's impossible to do and say the right things every time. You're only human, after all!

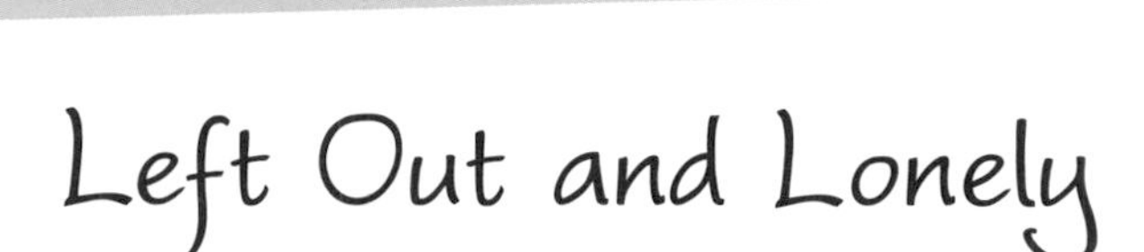

Left Out and Lonely

"There's always a positive spin you can put on things ... no matter how bad things are."

Jessica Ennis, athlete and Olympic gold medallist

Everyone feels lonely sometimes

Feeling alone isn't fun, and you can start thinking, "What's wrong with me?" But it's usually just the way things have worked out. Perhaps a couple of friends have started an activity and are spending lots of time together. Or maybe everyone's just preoccupied with things going on in their own lives. If there's no one to hang out with right now, think about how you can broaden your friendship circle. Maybe there's someone at school who seems shy – perhaps you could start chatting to them? Could you start a new activity like a sport or drama club? It's easier to get to know people when you have a shared interest. Try to be open-minded, too. Sometimes, you don't know if a person's likely to become a friend until you've spent quite a bit of time with them. Everyone deserves a chance and, the more friendly you are, the more people will be drawn to you. Remind yourself of all your positive qualities and you'll come across as a fun, generous girl who has time for everyone.

AGONY AUNT

Tackling your friendship dilemmas...

Q. I've found out that two of my friends went on a day out together. Why didn't they invite me?
A. Try not to take it to heart, as they probably just felt like doing something as a pair. Friends often do things in different combinations, and it doesn't mean they think any less of you. Next time, why don't you organize something with one of your friends?

Q. My best friend has started spending a lot of time with someone else. What should I do?
A. It's upsetting when you feel you're being replaced. The worst thing to do is accuse your friend of ignoring or dropping you - after all, sometimes you might feel like being with someone else too. Try to be your normal friendly self with her, but also get chatting to other people until you find someone you click with. You can't force your friend to spend time with you - but you shouldn't have to hang around by yourself either.

Q. I've found out that a bunch of my friends have been gossiping behind my back. How should I handle this?
A. People who gossip about you don't fall under the heading of 'true friends'. You need to be able to trust your friends, and feel that they're always on your side. It doesn't mean you need to fall out with the whole group, though. It's probably one person who's started it and the rest have just followed along. Just brush it aside and show that you're not bothered by a bit of silly gossip.

Q. I have two really good friends but I wouldn't say I'm really popular. Am I doing something wrong?
A. Not a bit. Where friends are concerned, things like loyalty, and genuinely caring for each other, are more important than sheer numbers. Some people like to collect as many friends as they can, but most of those aren't deep, meaningful friendships. Often they're just badges saying, 'Look how popular I am.' As long as you have someone to talk to, and who you can trust, then you have nothing to worry about.

Why the nicest people can act weird

People act out of character sometimes. Maybe your best friend has suddenly stopped wanting to spend so much time with you, or she's gone quiet and moody. It's natural to panic and think "What have I done wrong? Doesn't she like me anymore?" Yet, when a friend's behavior changes, it's likely that it's nothing to do with you at all.

Rather than ignoring her mood, show your friend you've noticed by asking if she'd like to get together. Perhaps you could invite her to your place so it's just the two of you. If you're worried about awkward silences, it's handy to have something to do (this can be as simple as trying out your new nail polishes, or asking her to help to rearrange your room). Then you could casually say something like, "This is nice – I've missed spending time together." If there's still a distinct feeling that you're growing apart, then gently distance yourself, while still being friendly when you see her. It's normal for friendships to change like this and sometimes, if you get on with your life and make new friends, those old friends drift back into your life again.

Feeling good about yourself

Of course friends matter – but it's important to believe in yourself too. Developing confidence means you can handle all kinds of situations, even when your friends aren't around. Yes, they're great for boosting self-esteem, but it should also come from within yourself. Friends who knock your confidence, and make you feel worried or insecure, aren't true friends at all.

Ten ways to make your confidence soar

1 ***Develop your talents.*** Whether it's art, music or sports, or something else entirely, devoting time to your passion will help you improve and enjoy it even more.

2 ***Setting goals*** is a good way to build self-esteem. Each time you reach one, push yourself a little bit further, and allow yourself to feel proud when you've done something well. Don't just sweep it aside and tell yourself it was "nothing".

3 ***Focus on your qualities,*** rather than dwelling on what you think of as faults. It'll help you make friends, too, as people tend to gravitate towards positive types.

4 ***While it's important to try your hardest,*** don't expect to be perfect or always number one. Your best is more than good enough!

5 ***If someone puts you down,*** ask yourself why they're doing it. It's usually because they feel insecure (confident people don't need to make others feel small). So just ignore them.

6 ***Remind yourself*** that, even when things don't go the way you would have liked, you can always learn something from the experience. And that'll make you feel stronger, and more prepared, next time.

7 ***Accept compliments*** with a smile and a thank you.

8 ***Helping other people*** gives you that warm, fuzzy glow of knowing you're making a difference. It's a great confidence builder too.

9 ***Sometimes, acting more confident*** than you really feel can make you braver. If you can get in a habit of doing this, it'll soon become the "real you".

10 ***Don't think, "I wish I was more like her",*** or try to model yourself on someone else. You're unique and amazing – there's no one else like you!

Wanted: new friends

Maybe you've moved to a new school, or feel it's time to shake things up and get to know some different people. Here's how to find some like-minded souls…

Try something new…

Try out new activities until you find something you really shine at. It doesn't matter if you've never thought of doing it before. Rather than thinking, "That's not for me" or, "I won't be any good at that", just give it a go. Straight away, you'll meet a bunch of new people.

Dare to go it alone…

It can be scary, walking into a new place without a friend at your side. But that's the hardest part – the walking in. When your best friend's beside you, it's tempting to stick together. But if you're on your own, you're more likely to start chatting – and you'll seem more approachable too (a tightly knit pair can appear slightly intimidating sometimes).

Befriend the new girl...

If she's just arrived at your school, she'll be delighted to see a friendly face. Offer to show her around and sit with her at lunch.

Don't judge others...

It doesn't matter if someone comes from a different background or culture, or if they seem to be into different things. When you take the time to get to know the real person, you'll often be amazed by how much you might have in common.

Be visible!

When you find yourself in a new situation, it's tempting to lurk in the corner so you're not noticed. But to make new friends, you really have to take a deep breath and make yourself visible. That doesn't mean being loud in a "look at me!" sort of way. It just means being warm, friendly and confident – the kind of person you'd look at and think, "I'd like her to be my friend."

Breaking the ice

So ... how to get talking to someone new? There are lots of ways to make that first move...

Smile and say "hi". Obvious, yes – but instantly, you'll seem approachable.

Ask a question. An ordinary one will do – "How long have you been coming here?" Or, "Do you know so-and-so?"

Give a compliment. Immediately, it'll make the person warm to you. Something like, "I love your bag, where did you get it?" will do just fine.

Find out what you have in common. You'll soon know if you've met a like-minded person you can get along with.

Don't take yourself too seriously. People tend to warm towards you when you show you can laugh at yourself. Plus, a person who smiles and laughs easily is always more fun than someone who looks serious.

If you're nervous, say so. Admitting it will make you seem likeable and honest – someone who's not afraid to show her weaknesses.

Take things slowly. Once you feel you've gotten to know someone, maybe ask them over to hang out with you, or arrange to meet up.

Relax and be you. Meeting new people is always a little daunting, and putting on an act can make it more stressful. Don't add to the pressure by thinking you have to be the funniest, wittiest or smartest person in the room.

Smart Girl Talk

I'm So Shy...

Even the boldest people feel shy sometimes. It's not always a negative thing either. Shyness can be really appealing – it's something people can relate to, as, chances are, they experience it too. If it's stopping you from making friends, try focusing less on yourself, and how exposed, embarrassed or alone you feel, and switch your attention to other people instead. Show you're interested by asking them questions and finding out about their lives – you'll soon forget about feeling awkward.

Why new friends are good for you

You might feel you don't need new people in your life but it's always good to be open to meeting different people. Friendships circles can become cliquey, and petty squabbles can make even your best friendships feel like hard work sometimes. Of course, you shouldn't dump your old friends. But inviting new people into your life helps to broaden your outlook. It keeps things fresh and interesting and more fun.

New friendship dilemmas

Five common scenarios – and how to make things work out…

Dilemma: *You've made a new friend, but your old friends don't like her…*

People can feel unsettled or threatened by change. Your friends were probably quite happy the way things were – then, *bang*, a newbie arrives and alters the dynamics. This shouldn't put you off making new friends, though. Just make sure you still have one-on-one time with your old friends, and reassure them that you're still there for them too.

Dilemma: *Your new friend has gotten close to another of your friends – and now they're leaving you out…*

So they're getting on a bit too well for your liking? A new person often has novelty value and everyone clamors for their attention. Don't just shrink back into the shadows – join in, be cheerful and make your voice heard. The new girl is probably just trying to fit in, and will be pleased to have more than one new friend.

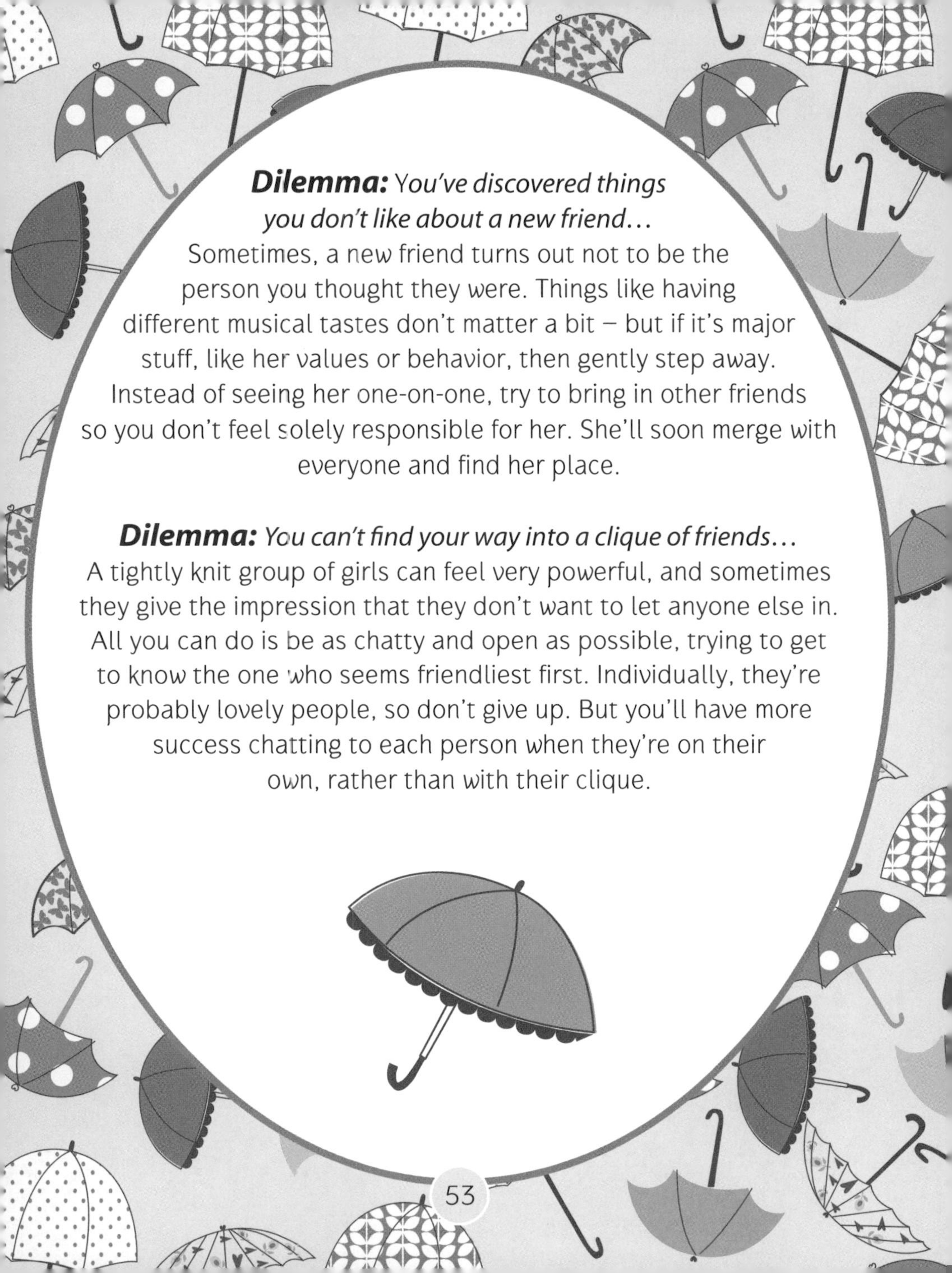

***Dilemma:** You've discovered things you don't like about a new friend...*

Sometimes, a new friend turns out not to be the person you thought they were. Things like having different musical tastes don't matter a bit – but if it's major stuff, like her values or behavior, then gently step away. Instead of seeing her one-on-one, try to bring in other friends so you don't feel solely responsible for her. She'll soon merge with everyone and find her place.

***Dilemma:** You can't find your way into a clique of friends...*

A tightly knit group of girls can feel very powerful, and sometimes they give the impression that they don't want to let anyone else in. All you can do is be as chatty and open as possible, trying to get to know the one who seems friendliest first. Individually, they're probably lovely people, so don't give up. But you'll have more success chatting to each person when they're on their own, rather than with their clique.

Being Friends with Boys

"Most of my friends were boys. I was such a tomboy. I enjoyed doing guy things."

Megan Fox, actor

Are boys' friendships different?

You know how much you love and need your friends around you? Well, it's just the same for boys. Like you, they want a sense of "belonging", and their friends help them to feel confident, happy and secure. Yet there are some differences too.

Have you noticed how girls can say mean things to each other, and have little squabbles and upsets? Boys tends to have fewer fall-outs, and the way they behave together is different too. Girls often wear their hearts on their sleeves, discussing their innermost feelings with their whole friendship circle. A boy might confide in a friend occasionally – but he's less inclined to "talk feelings" on a daily basis.

Boys also tend to spend their time together playing games or doing activities, whereas girls are often happy to hang out and chat. While they might "play rough", most boys hug and touch each other less than girls do – but they're just as loyal to their friends as you are.

Of course, there are exceptions. Some girls keep their feelings strictly private – and there are sensitive boys who don't go in for the sarcastic, teasing banter that their friends enjoy. So remember these are just generalizations and don't necessarily describe everyone. When you get to know boys as friends, you'll discover that they are all individuals, with their little quirks and special qualities, just like you.

Things some boys like doing…

Being competitive. A lot of boys feel it's important to be the best (the alpha-boy, if you like).

Making friends through their hobbies or interests – such as, football, swimming, music or gaming.

Messing around and teasing each other.

Showing off to get your attention.

Boys have worries too

You might think all boys are brimming with confidence. But they can feel just as worried and insecure as girls do – and for a boy, it can be harder to admit it. A lot of boys believe they mustn't admit to having weaknesses, and try to cover them up when they're feeling out of their depth. They might show off, say mean things or act up to get attention. It's important to remember that this kind of behavior is usually put on as a way of saying, "I'm fine!" It's worth talking the time to get to know the real person underneath.

Boy friend or boyfriend?

At school, people can seem obsessed about whether someone is your boyfriend or not. It can feel as if, as soon as you make friends with a boy, everyone's gossiping and giggling. The only thing to do is ... ignore them. Whether you want to use the label "friend" or "boyfriend" is completely up to you, although regarding someone as your boyfriend can make things feel more pressured than they need to be. It can also lead to jealousies if he (or you) starts spending time with someone else. Basically, a friend is a friend, whether they're a boy or a girl. So try to take the focus off their gender and just regard them as the unique, lovely person they are.

When you're being teased

If you're being hassled over your friendship with a boy, it's handy to have a few quick responses stored up in your brain. For instance, in reply to, "Is so-and-so your boyfriend?" you could just turn around and say, "He's my friend and he's a boy, that's all." When people tease you, they want a reaction. If you remain cool and unruffled, they'll soon give up and go off to pester someone else.

The main thing to remember is that being friends with a boy isn't a big deal. It'll happen more and more as you go up through secondary school, and people will stop seeing it as something to tease you about. It's totally up to *you* who you're friends with.

Help – I've been dumped!

When people start pairing off and having boyfriends, things can get a bit trickier. Being dumped by a boy can be upsetting – but try to keep things in perspective. At your school, there might be a craze for dumping people every five minutes. Sometimes, people don't even tell the "dumpee" themselves, getting a friend to do it for them instead. People can even find themselves competing to dump each other first ("I dumped her." "No, I dumped *him!*"). It's all a bit silly and unnecessary. If you do have a boyfriend, but don't want to be his girlfriend anymore, the kindest way to tell him is by saying you'd just like to be friends instead. You don't even have to use the D-word at all.

How to make friends with boys

A boy *can* be a girl's best friend – but how can you get to know one? The trick is to stop thinking of boys as different. There's no need to act flirty with them – it can come across as a bit odd, and be quite off-putting. Boys like girls who are natural, friendly and fun to be around. Just the kind of people you gravitate towards, in fact. Just like with girls, questions can be good conversation starters. Chat away and find out if you have any common interests. Keep the conversation light and jokey and you'll soon be chattering away like old friends.

More tips to try...

Do enjoy the fact that boys are less likely to care about things like hairstyles and clothes – they just want to get out and have fun. Of course you need your female friends, but it can also can be refreshing to do things that are less girlie for a change.

Don't forget that boys have shy-attacks too, just like you. However, most of them like getting to know girls, so if he's quiet, he might just be feeling self-conscious and not know what to say.

Do hang out as a big, mixed group sometimes. Welcoming a boy into the gang can change things, in a good way. For instance, you might notice that there are fewer intense discussions and gossip among the girls. Having a boy around can be like a breath of fresh air!

Don't view boys as a different species – they have the same hopes, pressures, fears and dreams that you do. If you haven't grown up with brothers, you might be a little unused to hanging out with guys as friends. It helps to remember that everyone is unique, and that a boy will have many aspects to his personality, just as girls do.

Do relax and be yourself – whether you're friends with boys or girls.

Ten reasons why boys make great friends

1 They can give you a different (and sometimes less complicated) point of view. Boys tend to analyze situations less than girls do.

2 They're often incredibly loyal to the people they care about.

3 You can usually trust a male friend to be honest, rather than saying what he thinks you want to hear.

4 Your boy pal won't steal your shoes. He might nick a dab of your lip balm, though.

5 If you're friends with a sporty boy, you might find yourself being more active too.

6 There are tons of things he can gain from your friendship that he doesn't get from his other friends. For instance, boys tend not to make a big fuss of birthdays, and they can be a bit reluctant to praise each other, too. So there's a lot you can do to boost a boy's confidence and make his world brighter.

7 If your girl group is acting a little fickle and weird, it can be refreshing to spend time with a nice, straightforward boy.

8 His tastes in music, movies and books might be different than yours. It's always good to have your eyes opened to new, unexpected things.

9 Your conversations will probably be different than those you have with your girlfriends. Variety keeps life fresh and interesting.

10 Boys are just fun to be around!

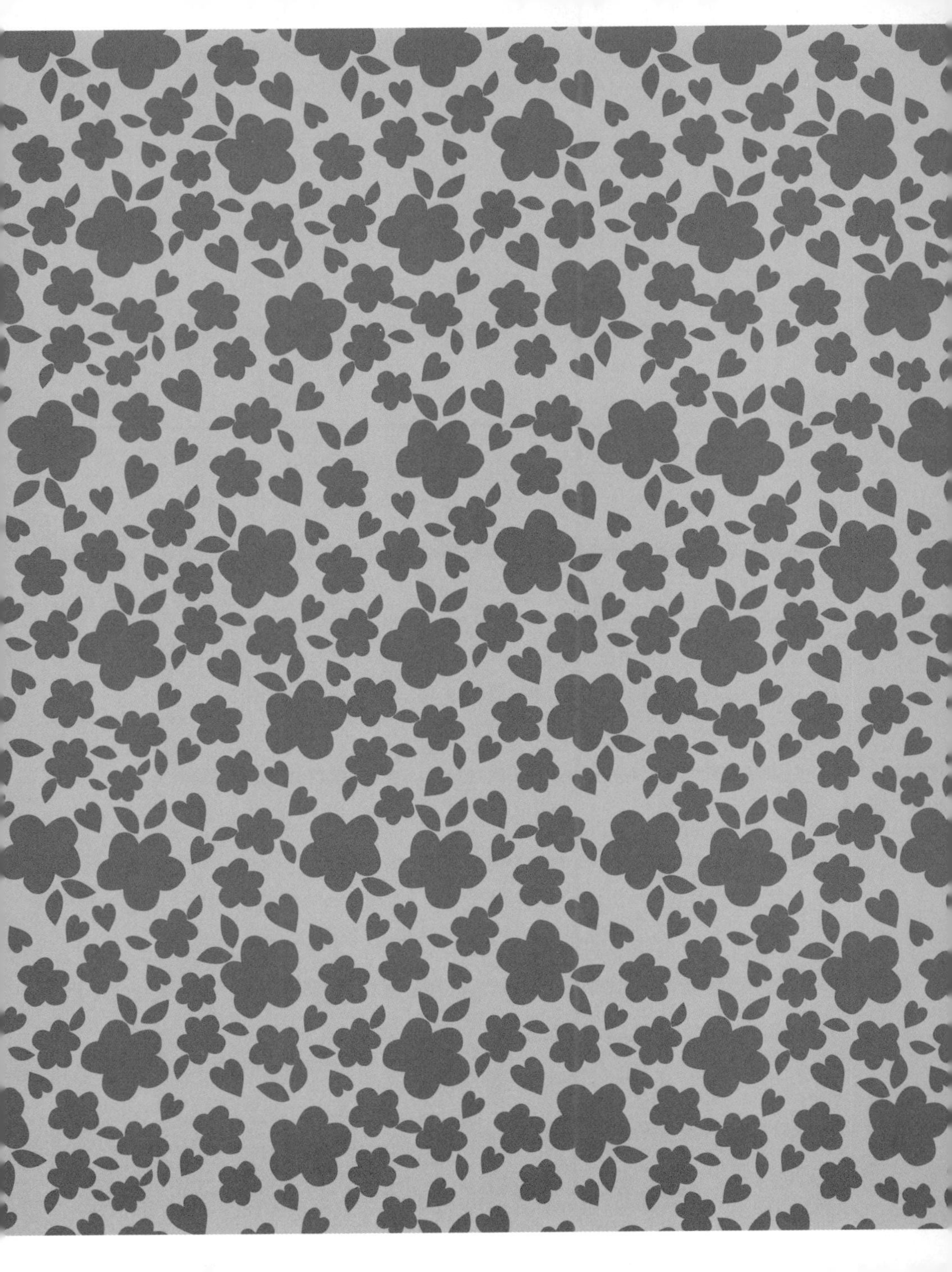

Growing Up – How Friendships Change

"The friends with whom I sat on graduation day have been my friends for life."

JK Rowling, author

Will we be friends forever?

Without a crystal ball, it's impossible to tell who your friends will be a few years down the line. All that really matters is enjoying being with the people you're close to, and doing all you can to keep those friendships as strong as you possibly can. So, when you agree with a friend that you'll be best friends forever, what you really mean is, "I'll do everything I can to make that happen."

Of course, while some friendships last a lifetime, others do fade away as you grow older. This might have happened to you already – remember that girl you played with when you were little, but hardly think about now? People move house or go to different schools, or their interests change and you no longer have so much in common. The thing to remember is that this is perfectly natural and happens to everyone at some point.

In fact, it's good and healthy for friendships to change and shift as time goes by. Human beings have a knack of seeking out the right friends for them at each stage of their lives. What's important is that you and your core group of friends – the ones who really matter – are always there for each other.

You're changing too...

Sometimes, you're the one who wants to change things around. Maybe you've met a new friend and love spending time with her. Meanwhile, an old friendship might feel stale – perhaps you don't have as much to talk about these days. But dropping someone is unkind and hurtful, so do make sure you still have time for an old friend, even if you've made new ones. If you feel you've really grown apart, you could still include her in group scenarios from time to time, even if you're not spending much one-to-one time together.

Will you still be friends in high school?

Changing schools can be testing time for friendships. Suddenly, there's a bunch of new people to get to know, and some of these are bound to become great buddies. You're no longer sitting in the same classroom for most of the day either, so you and your best friend probably won't see each other as much as before.

Instead of worrying, try to look at it as a new, exciting opportunity to broaden your circle of friends. Certain friendships might shift a little, but a true bond will stay strong. Plus, when you do get together at lunchtime or break, you'll have lots more to talk about.

AGONY AUNT

Handling those tricky changing times...

Q. My best friend and I used to have great times together. Now she just wants to talk about boys. What should I do?

A. When some girls start liking boys, they can seem pretty obsessed. Don't feel pressured to be like your friend - just keep doing the things you love to do. While you can still be friends, it's a good idea to get to know some new people who are more on your wavelength right now.

Q. I'm the first in my group of friends to wear a bra and am much more developed than everyone else. It's so embarrassing. Why has this happened to me?

A. Everyone develops at different times, and you can be sure your friends will all wear bras pretty soon. Have a word with your mom so you can make sure your bras are comfortable, pretty and give you a nice, natural shape. Focusing on other people, rather than worrying about what everyone thinks of you, can also help if you're feeling self-conscious.

Q. My mom's best friend has a daughter the same age as me. We used to get on, but now my heart sinks when Mom says she's invited her on a day out. Should I tell her how I feel?
A. Occasionally, you'll be expected to get along with someone like this. It's good practice for socializing with all kinds of people when you're older – at college, for instance. Have a word with your mom and say that, while you don't mind hanging out with this girl from time to time, you'd rather choose someone yourself for a day out. Your mom probably assumes you still enjoy being together as you got on so well when you were younger.

Q. Nearly all of my friends have started their periods. I haven't yet, and I feel so left behind. I just want to be like them!
A. Of course you want to share the experiences your friends are going through. There's nothing you can do to hurry things along, though – while some girls start their periods at ten, others may be thirteen or older. Although periods are nothing to worry about, at least you don't even have to think about them right now.

What do hormones have to do with anything?

You might have been feeling slightly "up and down" mood-wise lately – happy one minute and grumpy or tearful the next. Hormones, which are special chemicals produced by your body, make these changes happen. Remember, your friends are probably experiencing this too, which might help to explain things if they don't seem quite like their usual selves.

These mood changes are a normal part of the growing-up stage called puberty. This happens when your body starts to gradually change from a child's to an adult's. Your breasts will also begin to develop, pubic hair will start to appear and you'll have your first period. This is all natural and something every girl goes through as she approaches, or reaches, her teens.

Keeping your friendships on track

Ten ways to stay close and still have fun, no matter what life throws at you…

1 Is your friend supportive to you, and are you being as supportive as you can be to her? Everyone needs a **listening ear** sometimes. It might just take more organizing if you find yourselves in different classes or schools.

2 There's nothing wrong with saying **"I miss you"** if you feel you've drifted. Suggest a trip to the movies or a shopping afternoon – sometimes, a few fun hours together is all it takes to feel close again.

3 One of the great things about friends is that you know they're going through similar changes to you. It can be hugely reassuring to **chat about body issues girl-to-girl** with someone who understands. However, if something's worrying you, it's best to confide in a trusted adult too.

4 Some girls seem determined to keep in with the **most popular person in school**. Fine, if you genuinely get along – but if someone makes you feel insecure or unconfident, she's not the right friend for you. Instead, focus on those true friends who value you for who you are.

5 Try to accept that both you and your best friend will **make new friends** as you grow older and get to know more people. It doesn't mean she no longer wants to be friends with *you*.

6 Part of growing up is experimenting with clothes, hairstyles and make-up. Try to be helpful by making suggestions, and **resist teasing your friend** if she doesn't always get it right.

7 Growing up can feel stressful sometimes. If life seems intense, it's great to get together with your best buddy and do the kind of things you used to do together. Whether it's making a den or rolling down a hillside, sometimes it's great to **feel like a kid again** (and no one else needs to know...).

8 Oily, spotty skin is common during puberty and can knock a friend's confidence. Help her to choose the right products for her skin, and do all you can to **reassure her that she looks great**.

9 Friendship wobbles often happen towards the end of middle school. Your friend might be worried about the **big changes ahead**, so try to have relaxed, chilled-out times together.

10 **Don't blab to anyone else** if your friend talks to you about periods, other body changes or a crush. Instead, feel honored that she trusts you, and keep her secrets safe.

"Being popular was so much work! Do your own thing. As long as you learn that, you're cool."

Sandra Bullock, actor

Fact or fib?

Let's bust some friendship myths...

Myth: *You and your best friend should always agree*
If that were true, no one would have friends, because it's impossible to see eye-to-eye on absolutely everything. While it's important to have lots in common, it's also healthy to have different views too – that's what keeps a friendship interesting and alive. Just be sure to listen to her opinions and not dismiss them just because they don't match yours.

Myth: *You can't be best friends with a boy*
Yes you can. It's the person that counts, and what they're like as an individual – gender doesn't matter at all. If you come in for some teasing, don't let it affect your friendship. Boys need loyal, trustworthy friends just as much as girls do.

Myth: *You and your friends should be fairly similar people*
No – in fact, sometimes the strongest bonds are between people who are strikingly different. For instance, a confident extrovert often gets along great with a quieter type – those differences really complement each other. Often, a friend who's very different than you can bring out qualities you never knew you had.

Myth: *Everyone should have a best friend*

Perhaps you're not the "best friend type" and feel happier hanging out in a group. That's fine, and it doesn't mean there's anything wrong with you. In fact, as you grow older you'll find that the focus falls away from having a best friend. You'll probably have a whole range of friends, all with different qualities, ranging from the great listener to the one who always makes you laugh. Never feel pressured to choose someone as your best friend if you don't feel that way.

Myth: *Girls care about their friends more than boys do*

There might be more talk and discussion about female friendships, and it's true that they tend to be a little more complicated than the relationships boys have with each other. But that doesn't mean that boys need their friends less than you do. A boy is just as likely to be hurt, upset and even tearful if a friend is mean to him. He's just unlikely to show it, that's all.

Myth: *You should tell your best friend everything*

You might be the kind of girl who needs to share her innermost thoughts – or perhaps you're more private. There's nothing wrong with that, and a friend shouldn't pressure you to tell her things you'd rather keep to yourself. However, do bear in mind that talking over a worry can make it seem less huge. Plus, if you're very secretive, you might make it hard for others to get to know you.

Myth: *The more friends you have, the better*

Footballer David Beckham knows it's not a numbers game: "I'd rather have three very good friends than twenty good friends," he says. Of course, it's good to be friendly, especially when you find yourself in a new situation, like a different class. New friends make life fun – but you don't need vast numbers to be happy. Your core group is what really matters, as those are the ones who know you best.

Follow your heart

It's hard to pinpoint why you click with someone, but you know when it feels right. That's why it's important to trust your instincts when it comes to getting to know someone. Perhaps they have a different lifestyle, family background or beliefs. None of that matters if you like and want to friends with them. It's your choice, and it's always better to be guided by your own feelings, rather than what everyone else thinks. So be strong.

* A friendship motto to remember:

Follow your heart, not the crowd.

Where Would You be Without Friends?

"I love people who make me laugh ... it's probably the most important thing in a person."

Audrey Hepburn, actor

A friend in a million

What makes a star friend stand out from the rest?

- You can hang out together without talking, and those silences never feel awkward
- She doesn't try to change you, boss you about or make you more like her
- She thinks you're great just the way you are
- If you've done something wrong, she might gently suggest what you could have done instead. But she never judges you
- Sometimes it feels as if you can read each other's minds. That's why best friends don't have to explain everything to each other – they just *know*
- She knows all your favorites – from movie to song to ice-cream flavor, and everything in between
- She makes the most embarrassing moments seem funny
- Just half an hour of her company gives you that happy, just-had-a-warm bath kind of feeling
- You still feel close, even when she's far away
- It doesn't matter how busy she is. If you need her, she's there.

"She's amazing!" True stories of friendship

When a friend goes that extra mile for you…

Broken arm but still smiling...

"Last year, I fell off my bike, broke my arm and had to miss our Guides trip to France. When my friend Carrie found out, she asked her parents if she could come and stay with me for the week while the trip was going on. She lives hundreds of miles away in Devon but they arranged for her to fly to Scotland, where we live. We had the best week together, watching movies and chatting non-stop. It was so much fun, I no longer cared about my broken arm, or the Guides trip."

Beth, 13

Helping me through tough times...

"I'd been really upset because my mom and dad were breaking up. We'd had to sell my pony, Casper, because it was costing too much to keep him, and

I missed him so much. My best friend Nisha asked everyone she knew who had a pony if they needed help with mucking out and exercising, and someone nearby said they did. Their pony hasn't replaced casper but I've got to know him so well, he almost feels like mine."
Charlotte, 11

She made each day brighter...
"I have kidney problems and spent four weeks in the hospital last year. I missed my friends - and even school - but my best friend Kirsten cheered me up by sending a small gift nearly every day. Sometimes it was something she'd made, like a bracelet or a painted pebble. Or she'd write me a funny story or send me a piece of fudge. She visited too but, when she couldn't, those presents really made my day."
Jade, 10

She stuck up for me...
"Someone at school had set up a "Lucie Hate Page" on a social networking site and invited lots of people to join. I was so upset, but my friend Katy

reassured me that everyone thought it was pathetic. When we looked at it together, I saw that the posts were all saying things like, "This is so stupid - grow up." The whole thing actually made my other friendships stronger as I could see that so many people were on my side."
Lucie, 12

He helped me to fly (well, almost...)
"My best friend is a boy called Chris. He's a great runner and I love to run too, but I'm not as fast as him. We were doing a 5K fun run together and, although I was determined to do my best, I felt like my lungs were about to burst during the last five minutes. Among the big crowd of runners, Chris spotted me struggling. He slowed down to match my pace and ran alongside me, yelling, "Come on, you can do it!" Crossing the finishing line together was the best feeling in the world."
Megan, 13

And Finally ... Ten Great Things to Do with Your Friends

1 ***Have a fashion swap...*** So you've gotten tired of that top or those jeans? Your friends might love them, so dig out everything you no longer wear, asking your friends to do the same. Then get together for a trying-on and swapping session.

2 ***Make board games sweeter...*** Dig out a checker board and instead of the black and white counters, use sweets in two different colors. When you take a friend's piece, you get to eat it.

3 ***Make a magazine...*** Brainstorm ideas, decide who'll do what – then get writing – everything from stories, jokes and puzzles to celebrity features. You can stick in pictures cut out of magazines, or even take your own cover photo – starring you and your friends!

4 ***Have a carpet picnic in your room...*** Who cares if it's wet outside? Just ask each of your friends to bring something tasty, lay down a rug and dig in.

5 ***Predict her future...*** Make your friend a cup of tea by pouring boiling water over a teaspoon of loose tea leaves in a cup (you can rip open a tea bag for this – ask an

adult to help with the boiling water part, though). When it's cooled a little, she can drink (or pour away) her tea, leaving just a tiny amount in the bottom of the cup. Now get her to ask a question – such as, "Where will I go next summer?" and peer into the leaves to see what appears.

6 ***Design your own ice-cream sundaes...*** Plain vanilla is so much nicer when layered with fruit, crushed cookies and sweets in a tall glass.

7 ***Set up a blow-dry bar...*** All you need are your hairdryer, a water spray for dampening hair, and your hair products and accessories.

8 ***Make a movie...*** Think up an idea and draw a storyboard (the scenes where the main action happens). Decide on everyone's roles, then write a script or improvise. Get one of your friends to film your production.

9 ***Have a pyjama party in your room...*** Watch a pile of movies and be cozy in PJs and slippers all day long. Perfect for a wet winter's day.

10 ***Play "things I like about you"...*** Ask your friends to write down the three nicest qualities about each person (for instance, funny, caring, smart), then all read them out. In everyday life, we often forget to tell friends how much we appreciate them, so now's your chance.

Make your sleepover special

A little planning will make your get-together heaps more fun. Try these ten tips...

1 *Get the numbers right*

Four people is probably enough for that cozy feeling. Three can be a tricky number – you may need to make sure no one's left out.

2 *Where to sleep*

Avoid any squabbles by agreeing on this before your big night.

3 *Prettify your room*

Clearing away any clutter will make it more welcoming (you can store it in a box under your bed). Make up your bed with your favorite duvet cover and pillowcases, perhaps adding a fluffy throw or cushions for extra snugness. If you can, borrow lamps from other rooms for a low-lit, cozy feeling – much nicer than a dazzling overhead light. A string of fairy lights makes a room instantly girlie and inviting. Maybe there are some you could borrow from the Christmas decorations box?

4 *Theme it...*

For instance, watching scary movies and telling ghost stories makes an evening a real spine-chiller.

5 *Dig in*

Try making popcorn (let your friends add their own sugar or melted butter and salt), or have ready-made cupcakes that everyone can decorate. Pizzas are great to customize: set out mini bases, tomato sauce, salami, ham or veggies and grated cheese – plus whatever else you like – and get creative.

6 ***Time to make-up***

Try creating a completely different look for each of your friends, using the same three or four items of make-up. It's amazing how much you can do with a small selection of shades.

7 ***Manicures***

Try out different polish effects, from crackle to metallic to glitter. To avoid chipping and smears, it's best to allow nails a full 20 minutes to set hard (no matter what it says on the bottle). So perhaps plan your manicures for just before your movie, when you'll all be sitting still.

8 ***Share secrets...***

Or ask each friend to tell a surprising fact about themselves.

9 ***Midnight feast***

It's not a sleepover without one. Stock up on treats and see if you can hold out until the clock strikes twelve.

10 ***Look out for your friends***

Make sure everyone's happy, involved and having too much fun to feel homesick. But remember it's a good idea to have some quieter time when everyone can chill and relax.

Notes and Fun Ideas...